Marilyn

LOST IMAGES FROM THE
HOLLYWOOD
PHOTO ARCHIVE

Marilyn

COLIN SLATER

Captions & Commentary by
Boze Hadleigh

LYONS PRESS
Guilford, Connecticut

LYONS PRESS

An imprint of The Rowman & Littlefield Publishing Group, Inc.
4501 Forbes Blvd., Ste. 200
Lanham, MD 20706
www.rowman.com

Distributed by NATIONAL BOOK NETWORK

British Library Cataloguing in Publication Information available

Library of Congress Cataloging-in-Publication Data available

ISBN 978-1-4930-3343-0 (hardcover)
ISBN 978-1-4930-3344-7 (e-book)

♾™ The paper used in this publication meets the minimum requirements of American National Standard for Information Sciences—Permanence of Paper for Printed Library Materials, ANSI/NISO Z39.48-1992.

Printed in the United States of America

This is dedicated to Ronald Boze Stockwell and to Greg Schreiner.

—BOZE HADLEIGH

Contents

The Hollywood Photo Archive is not only a wonderful collection of cinematic history. It captures the collective memories of Hollywood. The gunmen, the gallants, the ghosts, and the stars of the big screen are represented in an impressive archive of more than 180,000 pieces.

The collection has been assembled over forty years by Director Colin Slater. In Slater's early days, as he began to learn his craft, it was the great directors, Wilder, Lean, and Welles, who advised him to study and learn from the film stills. Slater went on to own an important public relations agency, The Adventurers, in association with the legendary journalist and film executive, Fred Hift. Together with 500 stringers, the company worked on almost every motion picture produced and released in the U.K., gathering stills from the stars and press collateral from the studios. Added with Hift's lifetime of files, the Hollywood Archive was born.

The outstanding archive provides a treasure trove of prints for film buffs; delve in and discover wonderful film stills, celebrity portraits, and heroic stage performances. For more information contact wkdirections@outlook.com.

The Norma Jeane/Marilyn Monroe Photos

Many of the photos in this book were used by the studios to publicize their stars, particularly around the release of a new film. They would often be sent out to newspapers and magazines along with gratis movie tickets and a press release to encourage critics to write about the studio's latest releases.

These photos would include actual stills from the films, studio portraits in costume, film premieres, newsworthy events (like Monroe's performances in Korea before the troops), and even informal "candid" shots of actors between takes. After their use in the press, they were often not seen again, forgotten and/or filed away in some obscure studio backwater. Fortunately, the efforts of such collectors as the Hollywood Photo Archive have rescued hundreds of publicity photos of Marilyn Monroe, some which remain well-known, but many of which, such as the photos that follow, are just now being rediscovered.

The other genre of photographs used by the studios were costume tests, not generally circulated to the public but mostly used internally.

Finally, we celebrate Marilyn Monroe's early years with a cache of photos of Norma Jeane Mortensen (or Daugherty), from her infancy to just before she signed her first contract with 20th Century Fox. Before her fame grew in the 1950s, Marilyn had already appeared on dozens of magazine covers as Norma Jeane, a brief modeling career lost on all but the most ardent fans of Monroe's legacy.

A red circle, or halo, indicates the future most famous graduate of Emerson Junior High School, Los Angeles, class of 1940. Due to being a taller than average girl, Marilyn was sometimes cast in school plays as a boy.

NORMA JEANE

$\mathcal{M}$arilyn is an even bigger star in print," observed Hollywood columnist Louella Parsons, "than she is on screen."

The same holds true today. While millions have seen Marilyn Monroe's movies, billions have seen her timeless photographic images. Her rise to stardom, as well as her continuing global presence—which requires no translation—is largely due to her having avidly, almost obsessively posed for untold thousands of pictures, starting years before her first film contract.

Andre De Dienes, one of several lensmen who fell in love with Norma Jeane, believed "Her success would not have come about if she had not cooperated so whole-heartedly with many photographers."

As a model, a starlet, and a star, Monroe used still photographs more often than any other Hollywood luminary to further her career. Eve Arnold, the photographer Marilyn probably trusted most, said, "I never knew anyone who came close to her in natural ability to use both photographer and still camera." The screen idol's anxiety in front of the movie camera is well documented. Her relationship to the still camera was joyously opposite.

In the days when cameras were nowhere as prevalent or affordable as they are today, having your picture taken was something special. Norma Jeane yearned to be someone special and had the thwarted example of her mother to react against. Gladys Monroe wed at fifteen, had two children, then discovered her husband in bed with another woman one afternoon after coming home early from work (as a film cutter). Upon separating, he kidnapped their children. Marilyn later wrote, "My mother spent all her savings trying to get her children back.

"Finally she traced them to Kentucky and hitchhiked to where they were," living prosperously with their remarried father. Gladys "didn't ask him for anything, not even to kiss the children she had been hunting for so long."

She listed her children as dead upon entering the charity ward of the Los Angeles hospital where she gave birth to her third and final child, Norma Jeane, on June 1, 1926.

Emotionally disturbed and impoverished, Gladys gave Norma Jeane into the care of eleven foster homes, some of them relatives of hers, and one orphanage. She visited her daughter when she could, saved up to buy her piano lessons and fabric for new clothes, and hoped someday to reunite with her. Predictably, Norma Jeane was shy and lacked confidence. When the child addressed a foster mother as "Mama" the woman retorted that she wasn't her mother and not to call her that again.

In school Norma Jeane, dyslexic and a stutterer, didn't shine academically or socially, until she began to develop physically. At sixteen, before her latest foster family moved back east, she got married to avoid being remanded to an orphanage until age eighteen. Jim Dougherty wed her "because I was going into the service soon and I figured she'd have a home with my mother."

The bride took a war-time job inspecting parachutes. One day, a military photographer visited the factory and picked out Norma Jeane for color photographs, back when black-and-white was the norm. Corporal David Conover urged his photogenic subject to move into modeling and recommended her to the Blue Book Modeling Agency.

In well under a year Norma Jeane appeared on some three dozen magazine covers—more often than not in a swimsuit. Marilyn recalled, "I once asked why I had to wear a bathing suit for a toothpaste ad. He looked at me as if I was some kind of crazy!" The teenager also attended agency classes in posing, poise, grooming, and makeup. Blue Book made a short film of its rising model smiling into the camera in medium closeup, modeling a swimsuit, walking in a summer dress, and waving and smiling at the lens. Norma Jeane described it as the most exciting day of her life, so far.

Growing Up

Baby Norma Jeane in 1927. She was born June 1, 1926, in the Charity Ward of Los Angeles General Hospital to Gladys Monroe Baker Mortensen.

Norma Jeane's mother sometimes borrowed her daughter (here about age three) from her foster family for outings to the beach or the movies. After Gladys—a film cutter at Consolidated Studios—had to give up her first two children, her alcohol intake increased.

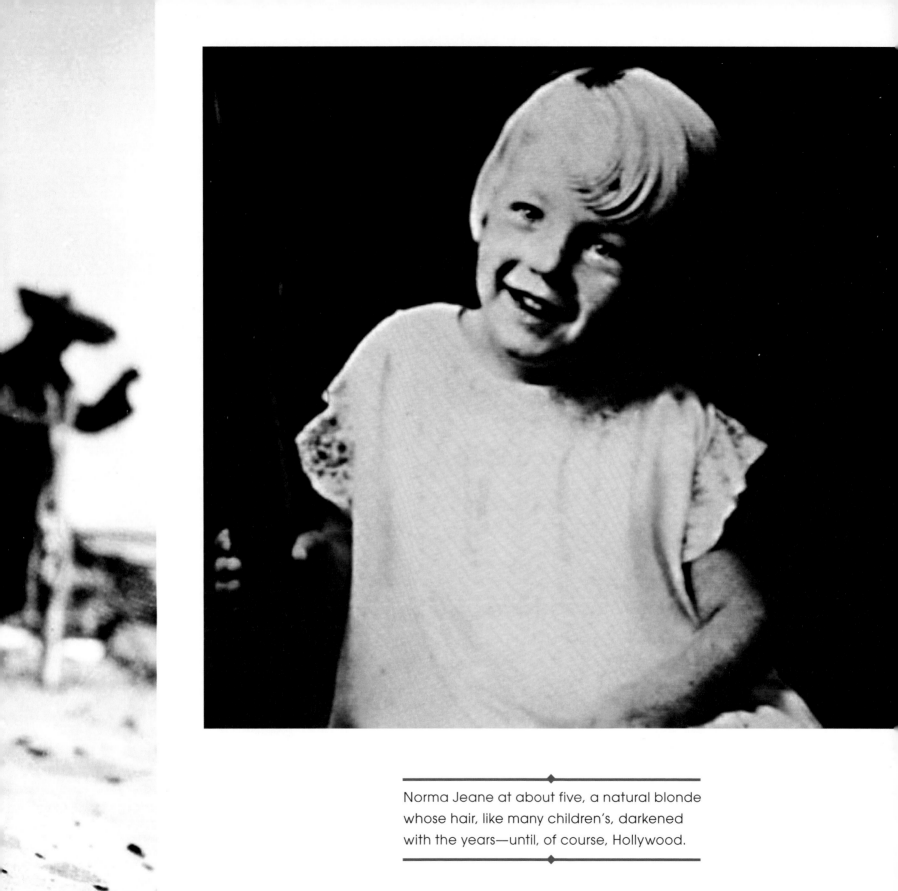

Norma Jeane at about five, a natural blonde whose hair, like many children's, darkened with the years—until, of course, Hollywood.

A very natural, even rural-looking Norma Jeane around 1940 in a photo originally given to a family member.

At Van Nuys High School in Van Nuys, near Los Angeles, Norma Jeane (far left, already smiling directly at the camera) was nicknamed "the Mmm Girl," partly because of her stutter, partly because she'd developed so quickly.

Norma Jeane in 1942, her assorted apparel unfortunately distracting from her face. The portrait was likely done in a local photo studio for her family.

This 1942 portrait illustrates Norma Jeane's surprisingly curly pre-Hollywood hair, noted by the Blue Book Modeling Agency's Emmeline Snively, who also reminded her client what the play said: Gentlemen prefer blondes.

Norma Jeane, photographed outside the Radioplane Corp. plant on June 26, 1945, by David Conover, overcame shyness and a stutter. She reportedly clipped a magazine item advising, "By acting confident, you will seem confident, and others' reaction will then instill genuine confidence."

The Blue Book Modeling Years

Newly signed model Norma Jeane, nineteen, was posed by photographer Richard C. Miller against an unobtrusive tree in this overly busy blouse.

The newly professional model and hopeful starlet confidently faces the future in 1945. To further the modeling career that would lead her to Hollywood, Norma Jeane used up all her savings and pawned her jewelry.

As a Blue Book model, Norma Jeane posed for a shampoo ad in 1945.

A Los Angeles native, Norma Jeane enjoyed posing in outdoor and rural settings. In autumn, 1945, photographer Andre De Dienes took her to a farm in the San Fernando Valley for a series of barnyard shots.

When she wasn't posing in a swimsuit, either Norma Jeane or her photographer often made some slight, sexy adjustment, as with her bared midriff in this shot by Transylvanian-born Andre De Dienes.

William Carroll shot the voluptuously innocent Norma Jeane at Castle Rock State Park in California in 1945, the year she signed with Emmeline Snively's Blue Book Modeling Agency. Within a year she became a leading pin-up model, initially in military magazines.

In one of her first professional photo shoots, 19-year-old Norma Jeane posed for Potter Hueth. Impressed by the young beauty, Hueth brought her to the exclusive Blue Book Modeling Agency in August 1945, and an exciting new career was born.

Marilyn didn't often wear red, a color deemed rather blatantly sexual at the time (as with the "adulteress dress" in *Niagara*). But in 1945 Norma Jeane sported what she called her lucky red sweater, no doubt hoping it might do for her what sweaters did for Lana Turner, the original Sweater Girl.

Andre De Dienes captured new model Norma Jeane (aka Jean Norman)
circa 1945 in an exuberant, innocent mood, with ruffles and pigtails yet.

For early photo sessions Norma Jeane sometimes had to supply her own wardrobe, as in this 1945 series by photographer Potter Hueth.

In early 1946 Richard C. Miller was one of the first professional photographers to shoot Norma Jeane, via the Blue Book Modeling Agency.

This wholesome photo of Norma Jeane, an animal lover, was taken by Andre De Dienes and made the cover of *Family Circle* magazine in April 1946. He also shot her with his dog, then used the result for a dog food ad.

Early on, photographer and sometime-beau Andre De Dienes liked to place Norma Jeane in natural settings, as in this 1946 shot in Death Valley, California.

Taken by Richard C. Miller in March 1946, for *True Romance* magazine. The then-Norma Jeane Dougherty wears her own wedding dress and clutches a prayer book belonging to Miller's wife. Ironically, Norma Jeane's first marriage ended in divorce a few months later.

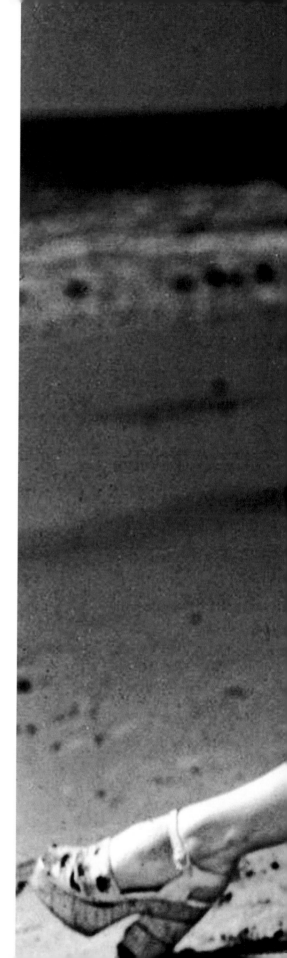

Laszlo Willinger photographed Norma Jeane by the seashore in 1946 (and also shot her in the same bathing suit indoors).

A photo from this wholesome session with the prolific Andre De Dienes wound up on the cover of *Family Circle* magazine.

Andre De Dienes did numerous cheese-cake shots of Norma Jeane in assorted bathing suits, including bikinis. The garment was named by a French designer after the Bikini Atoll where in 1946 an atomic bomb was exploded. The then-daring swimsuit was publicized as having an explosive effect.

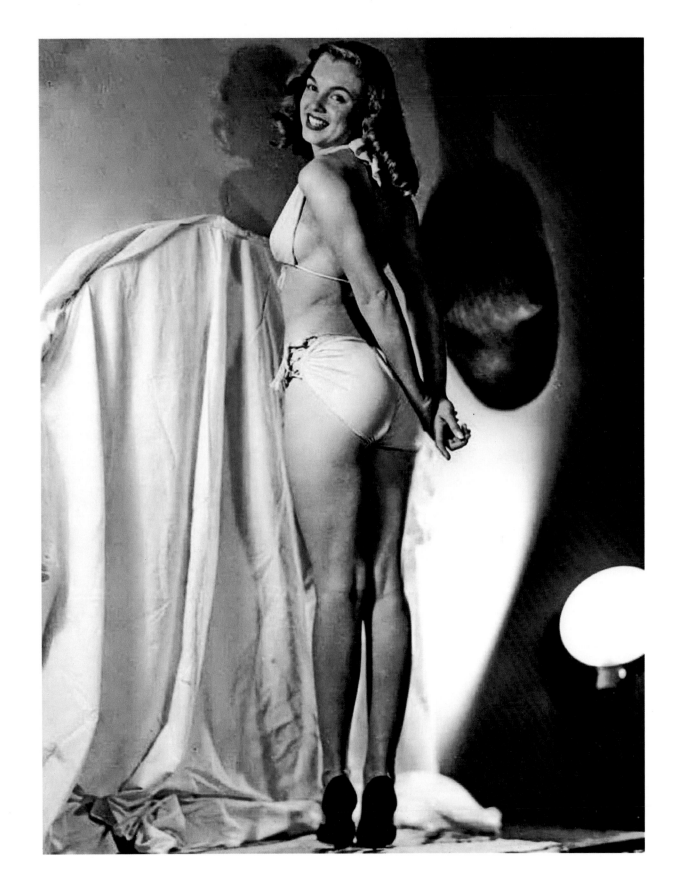

Among Norma Jeane's earliest assignments to help pay rent were $10-an-hour sessions for "girlie" illustrator Earl Moran. Between 1946 and 1950 she posed for photos that he rendered into illustrations for "gentlemen's" magazines. Somewhat surprisingly, he hired her through Miss Emmeline Snively's Blue Book Modeling Agency.

*B*ill Travilla, designer of several of Marilyn Monroe's most famous costumes, noted, "The public has little idea how much of a film star's time is consumed by wardrobe fittings and tests." Fortunately, Marilyn, who grew up with dresses that weren't often store-bought or fashionable, enjoyed changes of clothes and posing for wardrobe tests and movie stills.

Photos of wardrobe tests were never intended for public consumption, but were a vital, practical part of filmmaking. Too many have been destroyed, victims of corporate thinking that failed to value motion picture history. Those that remain are valuable esthetically and nostalgically. Some record outfits never seen in the finished movie, or barely seen, like Travilla's pleated gold gown, glimpsed momentarily from the back in a long-shot scene in *Gentlemen Prefer Blondes*. The stunning creation, which gilded the lily that was Marilyn, became infamous when she wore it to the 1953 Photoplay Awards and was criticized—by Joan Crawford, among others—for its plunging neckline, but then became famous via reproduction in myriad periodicals, its cleavage usually airbrushed out.

Early on, Norma Jeane began questioning photographers about how to yield better images. After she started posing for more indoor photos—rather than on the beach, at a farm, etc.—she developed an interest in lighting techniques. She adapted readily to the suggestion of Miss Emmeline Snively, owner-manager of the Blue Book Modeling Agency, that she lighten her hair back to blonde (her childhood color) for better photographic results.

As for makeup, Monroe became a master of the craft. Whitey Snyder, who did Marilyn's face from the start of her movie career up through her funeral, declared, "She has makeup tricks that nobody else has and nobody knows." Before turning twenty-four she'd studied *The Human Fabric*, a definitive book on anatomy by Andreas Vesalius that she marked in detail and, according to one biographer, "even at the end of her life would still instruct young friends with an encyclopedic knowledge of the human bone structure."

In 1946 Marilyn made the screen test that would result in her first Twentieth Century-Fox contract. Shot on the set of the new Betty Grable vehicle *Mother Wore Tights* by cinematographer Leon Shamroy, it was a silent test, due to the ex-model's lack of acting experience and her occasional stuttering.

Marilyn didn't take herself or her work overly seriously, for instance exiling other actors or crew from her sightline, as stars from Garbo to Faye Dunaway have done, or banning on-set visitors and press. Her most frequent costar, David Wayne, revealed, "Marilyn was friendly and sincere. She enjoyed meeting people, minus the Hollywood motivation of what can they do for me? When somebody talked with her, she genuinely listened."

Photos of the star between takes exhibit her candor, playfulness, occasional surprise or delight, and her ease when not performing for posterity for the motion picture camera. In any format, from wardrobe tests and movie stills to publicity shots and portraits, as well as between-takes pictures, Marilyn Monroe was and is a uniquely magnetic subject.

NEWMAN A635
MARILYN MONROE
AS "ROBERTA"
CH #2
EXT SCOTT
HOUSE-67,69

4/5/51   DES
         RENIE

Wardrobe test for *Love Nest* (1951). Extreme hats, severe outfits, and "hard" makeup gave way to a more natural and youthful look by decade's end.

Wardrobe test for *Love Nest* (1951), in which Marilyn plays Roberta, an ex-WAC who unwittingly causes jealousy in a boarding house.

Wardrobe test for *We're Not Married* (1952). The costumes were designed by Elois Jenssen, best known for garbing Lucille Ball in *I Love Lucy*. Marilyn plays Annabel Norris, a contestant in the Mrs. America (yes, Mrs.) beauty pageant.

Wardrobe test for *Niagara* (1953)—Marilyn as Rose in the controversial red dress. Her costumes for this film were designed by Dorothy Jeakins.

Wardrobe test for *Niagara* (1953). Photographer Joseph Jasgur felt the actress was particularly incandescent in white, "with the quality of a lightbulb."

Wardrobe test for *Niagara* (1953). The yellow raincoat was worn by female passengers aboard the Maid of the Mist tour boats that explore the falls.

Wardrobe test for *Gentlemen Prefer Blondes* (1953), costumes by Travilla. Despite playing Lorelei Lee, the titular blonde, second-billed Marilyn received a fraction of the salary costar Jane Russell did.

The text on the chalkboard in the image reads:

134
WILDER
MMONROE
AS
THE GIRL
XT. APT Window.
EVENING
SC. 55
CHG #7
DES. TRAVILLA
6/28/54

Wardrobe test for *The Seven Year Itch* (1955), for which Australian costume designer Orry-Kelly won an Academy Award.

Marilyn in what was probably a makeup or hair test for
The Seven Year Itch.

"Haven't you bothered me enough, you big banana-head?" Marilyn as Angela, fending off a policeman (Don Haggerty, father of TV's Dan) in the noir crime classic *The Asphalt Jungle* (1950).

Marilyn Monroe's most frequent screen character was a showgirl. In *Ladies of the Chorus* (1948), she plays Peggy, the showgirl daughter of another showgirl in the same chorus line.

Among distinguished company, Marilyn as Miss Caswell, a graduate of the Copacabana School of Dramatic Art, in *All About Eve* (1950) with Oscar winners Anne Baxter, Bette Davis, and George Sanders.

Marilyn as Peggy, a fish cannery worker, with costar Keith Andes in *Clash by Night* (1952), from a play by Clifford Odets and produced by gossip columnist Louella Parsons's daughter Harriet.

In her first lead role Marilyn portrays Nell, a mentally ill babysitter, in *Don't Bother to Knock* (1952). The film, which costarred Richard Widmark and newcomer Anne Bancroft, was not popular with audiences.

Marilyn and her *Clash by Night* (1952) costar Keith Andes, a rare blond love interest for MM (the film's starring love triangle comprised Barbara Stanwyck, Paul Douglas, and Robert Ryan).

Comprising five short stories by American writer O. Henry, O. Henry's *Full House* (1952) was titled *Full House in Great Britain*. Marilyn plays a nameless streetwalker who is thrilled to be called a lady.

Marilyn's "orange flame" gown *in Gentlemen Prefer Blondes* (1953) is obscured by this large, lavish, and unnecessary fur.

Marilyn as singer Sugar Kane in *Some Like It Hot* (1959), rehearsing with an almost all-girl band that includes Jack Lemmon and Tony Curtis.

SL(82-4)18

Marilyn in *Some Like It Hot* (1959), in a crowded train berth with four members of Sweet Sue's Society Syncopators.

Between Takes

Lauren Bacall, Betty Grable, and Marilyn Monroe on the set of *How to Marry a Millionaire* (1953), the first film shot in CinemaScope but the second to be released (the process was invented in France , then perfected by Fox).

Composer Irving Berlin with Marilyn Monroe, in costume for the torrid, much-criticized musical number "Heat Wave" in *There's No Business Like Show Business* (1954).

The bubblebath scene in *The Seven Year Itch* (1955) was closely monitored by Hollywood censors. Especially as it included the presence of an ogling male plumber.

During a break from shooting *The Seven Year Itch* (1955), with director Billy Wilder (standing) and visitor Sidney Skolsky, a leading gossip columnist who started championing Marilyn in 1950.

The Seven Year Itch (1955) director Billy Wilder with Marilyn Monroe in probably the most famous costume in film history. William Travilla's white halter dress was sold at auction in 2011 for $4.6 million, with an additional one million dollars paid in fees.

Wardrobe test: Marilyn as showgirl Elsie Marina in *The Prince and the Showgirl* (1957), the first and last film via Marilyn Monroe Productions. (Photograph by Milton Greene)

Marilyn checking her makeup as Cherie, an untalented singer in *Bus Stop* (1956), her first film since departing Hollywood to study Method acting with coach Lee Strasberg. The resultant reviews were among the best of her career.

Marilyn apparently doing a leg-lift on location for *Some Like It Hot* (1959). The looks- and weight-conscious star began working out regularly during her modeling days.

Director John Huston with Marilyn on the set of *The Misfits* (1961), whose original screenplay was written for her by then-husband Arthur Miller.

Like most actors of her era, Marilyn—seen here on horseback during Nevada location filming of *The Misfits* (1961)—had learned to ride a horse.

Marilyn Monroe and Clark Gable in *The Misfits* (1961), her last completed picture and his final one.

Marilyn being made up by her longtime makeup man and friend Allan "Whitey" Snyder and coiffed by Sydney Guilaroff. Snyder made up Marilyn's face after she died.

III MODEL

*L*ike other studies at the time, 20th Century-Fox expected its contract players to do any and all publicity requested of them. Never was a performer more cooperative than Marilyn Monroe, who took that name in 1946 (legally, in 1956) after Fox signed her and assigned her a new moniker. Cinematographer Leon Shamroy, who'd shot her screen test, stated, "Marilyn was canny and ambitious, yet child-like in her pleasure of costumes, posing and appearing in front of the (still) camera."

A big factor in Marilyn's willingness to, as it were, play dress-up and be photographed at her best was her childhood wish to become "so beautiful that people would turn to look at me…I dreamed of walking very proudly in beautiful clothes and being admired…and overhearing words of praise. I made up the praises and repeated them aloud as if someone else were saying them."

Norma Jeane must have intuited that her one route to fame and adulation was the camera eye into which she gazed so lovingly and often. Photographer Earl Leaf recalled a May 17, 1950, appointment to shoot the starlet. He used one roll of film and, satisfied, began packing up. Greatly disappointed, Norma Jeane "thought I was going so soon because it was no good. She pleaded with me to try a little longer.

"She said, 'I can climb trees, do hand-stands, cartwheels—anything you like.' And for twenty minutes she knocked herself out trying to give me original poses. I couldn't make her see it was unnecessary."

Norma Jeane/Marilyn exulted in each new magazine cover and enthusiastically did cheesecake, first as a model, then under studio contract. Though in time it became clear that Monroe was underpaid in relation to her value to Fox, the star realized publicity and maximum exposure were the key to increased public demand that would put pressure on her studio. So she complied, with little or no demur.

Because Fox had decreed their new contractee be (falsely) publicized as having been discovered while babysitting for a casting director, Marilyn was

To promote *Ladies of the Chorus* (1948), Marilyn posed in-studio for a series of "Los Angeles City Limits" shots by Columbia photographer Ed Cronenweth. Most of the stills featured MM in swimsuits.

photographed cheerfully diapering infants. In publicity for *Love Nest* (1951), Marilyn posed in a threesome featuring stars June Haver in high heels and William Lundigan as happily marrieds, with Monroe standing apart in unflattering shoes as a former WAC.

She did studio publicity in a gown already worn in *The Snows of Kilimanjaro* (1952) by actress Hildegard Neff. Some of those shots were used in print ads for beauty products like Westmore's "Close-up" lipstick and "Trueglow" liquid makeup—reportedly for minimal or no extra compensation.

A bona fide movie star by June 1953, while she was filming *There's No Business Like Show Business* (1954) Marilyn posed that month opposite Hedda Hopper in a childish costume with a tutu-like skirt while the gossip columnist, dressed with more dignity, presented her with the *Detroit Free Press*'s "New Faces Award," as if she were still a starlet.

By 1955, after her place in the stellar firmament was secure and following the huge success and worldwide publicity (the skirt-blowing scene) of *The Seven Year Itch*, Monroe had had enough. She demanded a new, fairer contract. Fox chief Darryl Zanuck replied he would sooner "destroy" Marilyn. So she left Hollywood for New York to study acting, a brave but much-ridiculed move. Fortunately her comeback in *Bus Stop* (1956), released almost fifteen months after *The Seven Year Itch*, won significant praise. Marilyn then became only the second actress to form her own eponymous production company; the first was silent star Mary Pickford.

Marilyn continued to engage in massive but well-considered publicity. However, just as she'd finally gained project and director approval, she could now choose her own photographers and means of self-expression. She explained, "When the photographers come, it's like looking in a mirror. They think they arrange me to suit themselves, but I use them to put myself over. It's necessary in the movie business." And Marilyn Monroe, the most famous female face of the twentieth century, certainly knew her business.

Studio Publicity Shots

Publicity shot by Ed Cronenweth for *Ladies of the Chorus* (1948). Marilyn's contract at Columbia was reportedly let go after she declined to spend the weekend aboard studio chief Harry Cohn's yacht. Like Fox's Darryl Zanuck, "Genghis" Cohn was widely known as a sexual opportunist.

In 1946 Marilyn was signed by Fox, which sometimes posed her in "social" settings (note the more formal makeup) for publicity. The studio dropped her the next year. Monroe signed with Columbia in 1948, then re-signed with Fox in 1951.

In the early 1950s women working out with weights was an unusual sight. David Cicero took a photo series of Marilyn exercising that was meant to catch the public eye—and did!

While making *Ladies of the Chorus* (1948), Columbia assigned Marilyn to be photographed for a partly cheese-cake piece on "How to Exercise."

Marilyn, demonstrating "How to Exercise," was already into calisthenics and jogging. In the early 1940s she studied weightlifting with former Olympic champ Howard Corrington.

As shown in "How to Exercise," Marilyn was athletic and flexible. She studied yoga with Indra Devi, who'd previously taught Greta Garbo and Gloria Swanson.

This 1948 color portrait was taken by John Miehle, a Hollywood still photographer who worked with Ginger Rogers, Carole Lombard, and others. His shots of Marilyn graced several magazine covers in the early 1950s, including *True Romance*.

Marilyn in a white terrycloth robe and a pensive mood on the beach, photographed in 1949 by Andre De Dienes.

Marilyn displaying a brighter mood, part of the 1949 beach series by Andre De Dienes, who'd fallen in love with 19-year-old Norma Jeane during a long modeling trip.

Fresh from a swim in the pool at Palm Springs, captured by Bruno Bernard in 1949. The desert resort was a weekend-getaway favorite of Marilyn's over the years.

A portrait of Marilyn at the time of *Love Happy* (1949), taken by J.R. Eyerman.

A portrait from *Love Happy* (1949), a "Mary Pickford Presentation" of a Marx Brothers comedy released by United Artists. Marilyn has a sexy-campy walk-on as an unnamed blonde. Groucho Marx deemed her a mix of Theda Bara, Mae West, and Little Bo-Peep.

Another *Love Happy* studio portrait. Marilyn reportedly supplied the gown (won via a modeling assignment) that she wore in her too-brief scene. The film ran out of money during production but was completed partially thanks to early product placement.

Laszlo Willinger's more
acrobatic 1949 jumping-
Marilyn photography
anticipates Philippe
Halsman's more famous
jumping pictures by
several years.

Following Marilyn's small but attention-getting roles in the 1950 films *The Asphalt Jungle* and *All About Eve*, Ed Clark photographed the future star for *Life* magazine.

At the Palm Springs Racquet Club in 1949 with boyfriend Johnny Hyde, whose marriage proposal she refused. A vice president of the William Morris talent agency, Hyde secured for Marilyn small roles in the major 1950 movies *All About Eve* and *The Asphalt Jungle*.

John Engstead captured Marilyn's soft yet alluring Miss Caswell look from *All About Eve* (1950). Biographer Lois Banner divided MM's makeup and looks into "hard Marilyn" (*Niagara, Gentlemen Prefer Blondes*, etc.) and "soft Marilyn" (this, and her 1960s pictures).

Marilyn, nicknamed "the Blowtorch Blonde" by gossip columnist Hedda Hopper, atop a doomed block of ice, dressed as an "Indian." Marilyn believed, "Cheesecake helps call attention to you. Then you can follow through and prove yourself."

Contrary to her screen image, Marilyn was an avid reader. Here, photographed by John Florea in 1951, she reads *How to Develop Your Thinking Ability* by Kenneth S. Keyes.

Starlet Marilyn Monroe in 1950. One columnist falsely claimed Norma Jeane was renamed after U.S. president James Monroe. The error was picked up and perpetuated by several periodicals and a few biographers. Another non-fact: that mother Gladys named her daughter after movie stars Norma Talmadge and Jean Harlow.

A 1951 publicity photo by Anthony Beauchamp. Unlike many sex symbols, Marilyn had few qualms about appearing in swimsuits or even less.

By 1951 boudoir cheesecake was old hat, a World War II remnant. Swimsuits, especially bikinis, were bolder and "in." However, Bruno Bernard, who photographed Norma Jeane from early on and became infatuated with her, had old-school tastes.

Marilyn graced photos set on west and east coast beaches. This California shot was taken by an Associated Press lensman on April 17, 1951.

Marilyn wore this polka-dot bikini in *Love Nest* (1951); however, her hair style in the movie was different.

Though she loved the beach and the sun, Marilyn the actress had to limit her exposure for her complexion's sake. A 1951 AP photo.

Another 1951 AP photo, this one with Marilyn facing inland.

Marilyn wore this ball gown on March 29, 1951, to present an Academy Award. After the ceremonies, pictures were taken at a photo fashion shoot. (Photograph by John Florea)

"Cowgirl" Marilyn posed for Valentine's Day publicity shots on February 13, 1951. The following year, she did a different (non-archery-themed) set of Valentine's Day poses for a name photographer.

A studio publicity portrait from 1952 or '53 illustrating Marilyn's belief that beauty was intrinsic but glamour could be easily manufactured. It was sometimes noted, more so after her death, that MM was a rare sex symbol who was also liked by women.

A 1952 shot from a Fox publicity series of Marilyn eating an apple, partly to promote her temptress role in the studio's *Niagara*.

Cheesecake shot taken by Fox photographer Frank Powolny to help publicize Marilyn in *Clash by Night* (1952).

Baseball, cheesecake-style, with Marilyn up at bat in July 1952, as part of the Twentieth Century-Fox Studio League.

In response to media criticism of her too-sexy gown at the Henrietta Awards in 1952, Marilyn posed in an Idaho potato sack for a widely reproduced photograph taken by Earl Theisen.

Marilyn and her *Gentlemen Prefer Blondes* (1953) costar Jane Russell set their handprints in cement at Grauman's Chinese Theatre on June 26, 1953 .

In 1953 Marilyn broke through to superstardom. As her fame grew, there were more portraits and headshots, less posing in swimsuits, less cheesecake. Said MM, modestly or ingenuously, "Pretty is just how good you apply your base."

Photographer Frank Worth captured Marilyn off the set of *How to Marry a Millionaire* (1953), wearing one of her more memorable costumes (designed by Travilla).

This 1953 photo of Marilyn lounging outdoors was taken in the Hollywood Hills for a furniture company. Early in her career MM appeared
in ads for a wide variety of products. (Photographer unknown)

This 1953 publicity photo showcased Marilyn in a dress previously worn by Hildegard Neff in Fox's *The Snows of Kilimanjaro* (1952). Studios often recycled costumes, and some of MM's were later worn by other actresses.

Marilyn sleeveless in black-and-white stripes, photographed by Ted Baron in fall, 1954, at a friend's garden on North Rodeo Drive in Beverly Hills.

Studio publicity shot of Marilyn at the time of her 1954 western *River of No Return*, costarring Robert Mitchum.

Sitting in her black Cadillac, Marilyn holds up a treasured lithograph of childhood hero Abraham Lincoln that usually hung above her bed. Photographed in Los Angeles by Milton Greene in May 1954.

Publicity shot for *The Seven Year Itch* (1955) with Marilyn's admiring costar Tom Ewell. After this film, in which she played The Girl, Monroe departed Hollywood for New York and the Actors Studio, with the aim of more serious roles.

While in England filming *The Prince and the Showgirl*, Marilyn was photographed by Cecil Beaton, portraitist to the royal family. More widely reproduced than this shot was Marilyn in front of a Japanese wall hanging.

Cecil Beaton, at one time the world's highest-paid photographer, shot Marilyn at the Ambassador Hotel in New York City in 1956.

Marilyn was known to photographers as a willing, carefree, unself-conscious camera subject, unlike many actresses whose fame rested on their looks. This seemingly candid shot from circa 1956 is unusual in that it's a profile shot.

Pensive photo with ferns shot by Cecil Beaton on February 22, 1956. Beaton earned three Academy Awards for his film design work.

Monroe befriended
photographer Sam
Shaw in the early
1950s via a director
friend (the model-
turned-actress knew
how to network).
In 1957 Shaw shot
the Blue Dress series
near Marilyn and
Arthur Miller's rented
beach house at
Amagansett, Long
Island.

Marilyn, seen here in the 1957 Blue Dress series, was comfortable being photographed in natural as well as artificial settings. Lensman Sam Shaw noted that few actresses were willing to be captured in natural light.

Publicity photo of Marilyn taken in 1957 by Milton Greene, who during four years in the mid-1950s did fifty-two sessions with her. Like numerous Monroe stills, this one became a collectible movie card.

To help promote
*The Prince and the
Showgirl* in 1957,
Richard Avedon shot
a glamorous series
of Marilyn in a sheer
fur-trimmed cape
and sequined gown
(not part of her film
wardrobe). One shot
appeared on the
cover of the *New
York Mirror,* others
in *Life* and assorted
American and Euro-
pean periodicals.

Beautiful ruffled color portrait of Marilyn in *The Prince and the Showgirl* (1957), costumes by Beatrice Dawson, photo by Milton Greene.

The last publicity shots ever taken of Marilyn Monroe by 20th Century-Fox were for *Let's Make Love* (1960), in which she plays Amanda, a showgirl. In most foreign markets it was titled *The Millionaire*, after the character played by MM's choice of male lead, French star Yves Montand.

Six weeks before her death Marilyn did a photo shoot for *Vogue* magazine, part of her campaign to counteract negative publicity about her physical and mental fitness after being fired by her studio, Fox. Photographed by Bert Stern, the results became known as The Last Sitting.

On February 8, 1952, Marilyn received a Henrietta Award for Best Young Box Office Personality at Santa Monica 's Club Casa Del Mar, in a ceremony organized by the Hollywood Foreign Press Association. Her revealing gown was designed by Oleg Cassini, husband of actress Gene Tierney. (Photo by Earl Leaf)

*D*espite or due to becoming a top pin-up with a multitude of magazine covers behind her, Norma Jeane's ascent in Hollywood wasn't a fast one. Nor totally gratifying. She aspired to being taken seriously and expanding her image, both of which the studio system frowned on. Though her early screen roles were simply decorative, Marilyn continued working behind the scenes to enhance her future, professionally and personally.

"She was a great one for self improvement," said author and friend Leo Rosten. "She read voraciously, multiplied her vocabulary…and typically preferred a night in, with a book, to painting the town."

Emmeline Snively, who gave Norma Jeane her first modeling job at her Blue Book Modeling Agency in 1945, asserted, "Girls ask me all the time how they can be like Marilyn Monroe, and I tell them if they showed one tenth of the hard work and gumption that girl had, they'd be on their way."

Once Marilyn Monroe became a household name, each studio, including her own, offered the public blonde imitations and rivals. None of them "took," for Marilyn wasn't a type, she was a *sui generis* star. Upon joining the celluloid pantheon, Monroe reveled in it, as illustrated in photos and film of her at premieres, charity functions, and other social appearances. "She loved the limelight but didn't dwell in it," offered friend and fellow actress Susan Strasberg. "For Marilyn, that was a treat, showing up and being ogled. It wasn't a regular requirement for her ego."

Marilyn on the town was more in photographic evidence during the mid 1950s. With time and accelerated fame, she focused more on her private life.

However, she always remembered her Korean tour in February 1954—not long after the war ended there—as a highlight of her life. While honeymooning with Joe DiMaggio in Japan, Monroe was invited by the USO to entertain servicemen stationed in Korea for four intensive days. The troops and the showgirl got on like a house on fire. Acting or singing, she'd never performed live before large groups, let alone ten thousand at a time. The fervid reception that always greeted her inspired and touched Marilyn, who felt deeply for the men, far from home and loved ones, and in a very un-California-like climate.

She took extra time to chat with the soldiers and be photographed with them, to give autographs, trade jokes, view photos of their families, and even agree to write letters home for them. Korea, said Marilyn, was the first time she felt she had an impact on people and could cheer, even console them.

Marilyn always felt more comfortable with individuals than institutions. The media, for instance, often criticized the slight weight gain seen in her three final films. A gall bladder operation helped her slim down and appear— in the uncompleted *Something's Got to Give*—as beautiful as or even more so than ever, during the final months of her life. It was an apotheosis. Norma Jeane had transcended mere stardom; on August 4, 1962, Marilyn Monroe became a goddess.

With Ronald Reagan, attending a birthday party for her *Gentlemen Prefer Blondes* (1953) costar Charles Coburn on June 17, 1953, at the Beverly Hills Hotel.

Marilyn with Lauren Bacall and radio emcee at the 1953 premiere of *How to Marry a Millionaire*.

Marilyn at Ciro's nightclub in Hollywood (now the Comedy Store) with her How to *Marry a Millionaire* (1953) costar Lauren Bacall and Bacall's husband, Humphrey Bogart, following the film's premiere.

Marilyn Monroe and costar Donald O'Connor attending the premiere of *There's No Business Like Show Business* (1954).

Joe DiMaggio, Marilyn, and David Wayne on September 13, 1954, backstage after a performance of the Broadway hit *The Teahouse of the August Moon.* (Brando played the Okinawan Sakini in the film version.) Wayne and Monroe had already done four films together; he was her most frequent costar.

Reading publicity material for *East of Eden*, starring James Dean. Marilyn served as a celebrity usher at the film's March 9, 1955, premiere, a benefit to raise funds for the new home of the Actors Studio.

Dancing with Truman Capote at El Morocco in New York City on March 24, 1955. The author of *Breakfast at Tiffany's* later voiced his preference for Marilyn Monroe over Audrey Hepburn in the role of Holly Golightly. He admitted giving the character some of Marilyn's characteristics.

Marilyn is shown the finer points of a painting by her director Billy Wilder, sometime in the late 1950s.

Marilyn and Marlon Brando, costumed and clowning, publicizing the benefit premiere of the 1955 film of Tennessee Williams's *The Rose Tattoo* on behalf of the Actors Studio, photographed by Milton Greene.

Although they dated and made a stunning couple (but never worked together), Marilyn Monroe more than once denied having an affair with Marlon Brando. Seen here, probably in 1956, they met on the set of *Desiree*, in which the Nebraskan played Napoleon.

Marilyn with her third and last husband, Arthur Miller, in 1956. They met in Hollywood in 1951 but began a serious relationship in New York City in 1955.

Marilyn opens the soccer season at Ebbets
Field in Brooklyn, New York, on May 12, 1957.

Marilyn at Costello's
restaurant and bar in
New York City in 1958,
viewing wall art by
cartoonist-humorist
James Thurber.

On March 5, 1962, Rock Hudson escorted Marilyn to the Golden Globe Awards, where she was named 1961 female World Film Favorite.

Korea

Marilyn arriving to visit American armed forces, Seoul City Airport ,
South Korea, on February 17, 1954, photographed by Walt Durrell.

Some of the media accused Marilyn of performing for self-promotion. Those with her in Korea countered the absent critics; some mentioned her fear of disappointing audiences, as live performance of any kind was not Marilyn Monroe's forte, let alone before groups of 10,000 at a time.

Marilyn enjoyed interacting with the troops, giving extra time, talking and joking with individuals, even agreeing to write letters home to their loved ones. Several of their mothers wrote back to Marilyn.

Due to the rigors of the intensive four-day schedule in Korea, Marilyn reportedly contracted pneumonia. But she would look back on the experience with a mixture of joy, pride, and empathy for the service men she met there.

Marilyn gave her considerable all in ten shows for an estimated 100,000 servicemen, appearing on stage in summery clothes in temperatures that averaged 30 degrees Fahrenheit.

Performing live before huge, appreciative audiences helped diminish Marilyn's stage fright. Her tour was also a respite from Joe's jealousy and controlling behavior. Eight months later the marriage was over.

Celebrities entertaining servicemen was nowhere as common or safe an event—nor were television specials made out of them—in the early 1950s as later during the Vietnam war. Most stars who entertained "the boys" in the 1940s and `50s did so safely and comfortably at USO canteens back home.

"I never thought I had an effect on people until I was in Korea ," Marilyn later recalled. Some soldiers waited seven hours in the cold to get front-row seats to see Marilyn Monroe.

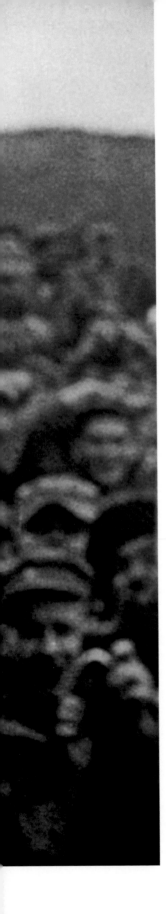

"Of all the performers who came to us in Korea…she was the best," said Ted Cieszynski, an Army Corps of Engineers photographer. He praised Marilyn's sincere friendliness to photographers and servicemen—soldiers and officers alike. "It was bitter cold, and she was in no hurry to leave."

"(It) was the best thing that ever happened to me," Marilyn declared about her Korean tour. "I never felt like a star before in my heart. It was so wonderful to look down and see a fellow smiling at me."